Hilda's

Verses

Hilda Petrie-Coutts

Copyright © Hilda Petrie-Coutts 2024

All Rights Reserved.

CONTENTS

THE OLD VIOLINIST	8
THE EMPTY GLEN	12
WRAITH OF BOWMERE'S LAKE	20
GREY WOLF	27
THE BALLET SHOES	33
THE FLOOD	39
GREEK ISLAND	48
POPPY IN THE CORN	53
JUANITA	60
THE MISSING BRIDE	63
THE MOOR	70
THE GREAT GLEN	76
JUNGLE RESCUE	79
THE BRIDGE	84

THE HARPIST	88
THE SNOW MELTS	98
THE CHOIR	100
THE CONCERT	105
THE POOL	111
ORD OF THE SPRING	116
CHARLES EDWARD	118
ODE TO BARNABY	124
DANCE THE NIGHT AWAY	126
ABENA	129
AFTERMATH	139
CANDLE TO RUDI	147
SKYE MEMORIES	149
DRUMBEAT OF LOVE – TO BYRON	152
THE VISION	154

MOTH IN A MOONBEAM	157
SKYE COTTAGE	159
THE CHRISTMAS TREE	162
MOONDUST	165
RIDERS IN THE NIGHT	167
EDINAMPLE COTTAGE	178
HYMN OF PRAISE	183
ROCK MY DARLING, ROCK	186
STORM CLOUDS	188
GOING HOME	189
ONLY A MAN	191
TARMACHAN RIDGE	194
THE THORNBUSH	196
THE BALALAIKA	198

THE OLD VIOLINIST

Wistful as chime of midnight bells,
Borne on the sands of time,
The silvered cadences arise,
Wild to the wind's acclaim.

They soar around that timbered cot,
Moss thatched o'er oaken beam,
Where an ancient violinist snores,
And turns in fitful dream.

A manuscript lies on his bed,
His pen beneath a chair,
Thrown with frustrations fevered aim,
Born of a life's despair.

His un-shuttered casement floods with light,
Lent by a radiant moon,
As strange, bewitching liquid notes,
Vibrate his lonely room.

He stirs and rubs his sleep filled eyes,
As there pours on startled ear,
Sweet wildly lilting, tender chords,
Now soaring rich and clear.

He struggles upright in his bed,
Fear stamped across his face,
Then staggers to unsteady feet,
Drawn by the music's grace.

Then stands transfixed in sudden awe,
To see his violin,
Bowed by angelic unseen hand,
Tucked neath an unseen chin.

The strings explore that elusive theme,
Which he in vain has sought.
The secret of a lifetime's quest,
Now in a moment caught.

The old musician gasps with joy,
Grasps pen in trembling hand.
Captures in ink those beauteous chords,
Which through his brain expand.

A final note, exquisite, sad,
Wings quivering to the sky.
The angel gently lowers the bow
And puts the violin by.

The old musician grasps the bow,
And draws it o'er the strings,
As once again the music flows,
And soars on magic wings.

The triumph, too great for his heart,
He staggers to his bed.
His violin splinters to the floor,
He falls—triumphant---dead.

A mighty wind blew through that room,
Those note filled sheets plucked forth,
In upward spiral with his soul,
Not to be read--on earth!

Dedicated to my dear daughter Tania, with love.

THE EMPTY GLEN

In an eerie, smoke filled twilight,
He ventured through the glen,
So quiet now, all cries had ceased,
Place quite devoid of men.

His factor had informed him,
The work had been well done,
Now he returned from city's lights,
To see what he'd begun.

The smell of smoke still lingered,
Last embers glowing still,
The ruined cots now roofless stood,
At his entrenched will.

He'd not wished to observe it,
Such infamy in his name,
Perhaps within his lordly heart,
Some shred remained of shame.

For centuries this glen had rung,
With laughter and with song,
Despite the hardships of their lives,
His folk were brave and strong.

Whenever their chief called them,
To rise and take up arms,
His men flocked to his banner,
Left wives, children and farms.

The chief was father of the clan,
They his loyal family,
All lived in mutual respect
Had through countless centuries.

Then came Culloden's blood soaked field,
Retribution in its wake,
As harsh and unforgiving foe,
The highlands sought to break.

Tartan made illegal,
The pipes and Gaelic too,
While the chief became a landlord
Ever tightening the screw.

His tacksmen and the cottars,
Struggled to raise high rents,
However hard the times became,
Nought could their courage dent.

Invited down to London,
Lairds wore velvet now and lace,
Gambled, fornicated, drank,
Behaviour a disgrace.

But such pleasures needed money,
English friends offer advice,
The lairds with keen receptive ears,
Accept it in a trice.

A rumour then began to spread,
Disturbing thought and sleep,
Lairds dispossessing tenants,
Replacing them with sheep.

A rash of black faced Cheviots,
Sweep across each hill and glen,
Their busy jaws and restless feet,
Displacing highland men.

While heroes serve their country,
In many a foreign field,
Mothers, wives and children weep,
To factor's henchmen, yield.

Down come the beams and timbers,
Thatched roofs collapse in flames,
Chairs, table, beds and spinning wheel,
All smashed in fulsome game.

Those resisting, savage beaten,
Forced to sleep beneath the sky,
Neighbours face the self same fate,
If to succour friends they try.

No matter what the weather,
Be it snow, rain, lashing sleet,
No shelter as these helpless ones,
Wander on hapless feet.

Many die of famine, sickness,
The stronger reach the shore,
Attempt a life as fishermen,
Face surging billows roar.

The laird walks through this latest glen,
To suffer fruits of clearance,
A cold discomfort fills his heart,
Peoples wholesale disappearance.

But his fellow lairds are gleeful,
Their coffers now are filling,
What loss impecunious crofters,
Milkmaids lilting at the shieling.

Destitute and helpless,
Thousands forced to emigrate,
To unknown lands across the seas,
In God alone now trust their fate.

The highlands and the islands,
Left empty now and bare,
The land despoiled of people,
Still echoes their despair.

What though hearts were breaking,
For the peat smoke in the glen,
For heather moor, deer on the hill,
They resolve to start again.

Yes, they brought their skills and courage,
Their Gaelic and their songs,
To many far off nations,
Where they now glad belong.

While here a curious tourist,
May sometimes ponder why,
Such beauteous land lies empty,
Under accusing sky.

Soaring mountains pierce the clouds,
Sides laced with waterfalls,
Mysterious lochs deep dreaming lie,
As swooping eagle calls.

Perhaps a clue may yet be found,
In low ruined walls of stone,
Where bracken and the heather spring,
To wind's soft grieving moan.

For a country to be despoiled
Of its people at the will,
Of cruel, rich and greedy men,
Such memory yet holds chill.

A few wealthy landowners,
Still hold the land in thrall,
Have turned it into deer parks,
Sheep bleat, grouse plaintive call.

I've heard a new term now exists,
For peoples cruel dispensing,
If I have got it juist aright,
They call it ethnic cleansing!

WRAITH OF BOWMERE'S LAKE

The demoiselle was very fair,
Within that woodland glade.
Bending low upon her knee,
Her hood slipped back and I could see,
The beauty of this maid.

Her hair was spun of fairy gold,
Her eyes of polished jade,
One hand caressed an ancient stone,
As from her lips came gentle moan,
Beneath that dappled shade.

'Now rest you soft my own true love',
Her voice was low and sweet.
She sprinkled flowers upon the mound,
That scarred once crudely ravaged ground,
Then rose back to her feet.

I moved, a twig snapped and she turned,
Eyes wide with sudden fear.
'I prithee stand thou back, Sir Knight,
In pity honour my sad plight,
No place for strangers here.'

'A stranger I'd no longer be,
I pray thee have no fear.
As knight my devoir offer thee,
To aid you shall my duty be,
Fair maid be of good cheer.'

My casque I lifted from my head,
The wind took beard and hair.
Her eyes to the escutcheon strayed,
So boldly on my shield displayed,
Her cry, one of despair.

'Thou art of that accursed house,
Whose hands with blood are red.
From Holy War my love returned,
Found family scattered, Castle burned,
Now my true knight lies dead.'

I stared at her bewildered for,
Some fifty years had passed,
Since men returned from the crusade,
The time my family's fortune made,
John's bounty unsurpassed.

This maid was troubled in her mind,
No doubt grief had dismayed her.
I reached a reassuring hand,
As hard I tried to understand
How time it seemed betrayed her.

Her flesh was cold to my quick touch,
She turned and fled before me.
Her feet no slightest sound did make,
Progress so light no bush did shake,
As soft cry did implore me.

'Begone, Sir Knight, no further come'
Her sobbing tones soft threatened.
Now sunset faded into night,
Before us gleamed dull, silver light,
Where Bowmere's Lake deep beckoned.

Her feet were gliding twixt the reeds,
That darkly fringed the water.
My hand closed upon empty air,
The demoiselle no longer there,
My eyes now vainly sought her.

I spent the night upon the bank,
Vain searching for the maiden,
Once I thought I heard her cry,
Yet mayhap 'twas the night winds sigh,
With sorrow deeply laden.

Morning dawned, lake glittered flame,
Around me was no other.
An otter splashed out from the bank,
Heron swooped low, legs long and lank,
Startled deer took cover.

I shook my head in troubled thought,
Retraced my steps back through the trees,
Paused before that lonely grave,
With fading wild flowers lightly lathed,
Stared down at them, with deep unease.

I bent, took up a fragrant bloom,
Raised it to lips with reverend care,
No dream these flowers lightly displayed,
Within this secret woodland glade,
But placed there by that maiden fair.

My grandsire warmed his ancient limbs,
Before the log fires roaring flame.
I told him of my ghostly tryst,
The maid who vanished in the mist,
'Elaine,' he said, 'that was her name.'

I learned her knight was foully slain,
By one who bore our family name.
Though he fought at Coeur de Lion's side,
Returned, was dispossessed and died,
To our family's deepest shame.

'Grandson, great lands you will inherit,
Due to an action once I made.
King John, his brother long despised,
So Richard's followers he surmised,
Were better dead, 'twas so he bade.'

'This Knight, Sir Edmund of Verunne,
Estates were forfeit on his return,
Him we slew, secretly buried,
Across the lake his body ferried,
Within that wood he was interred.'

'This crime committed by your hand?'
'You profit by it boy,' he jeered.
'I heard that his intended bride,
Had found his grave and daily plied,
That woodland with her futile tears.'

'They say she walked into the lake,
Her silly female pain to quench.'
I looked upon his wrinkled face,
Knew I now shouldered his disgrace,
'Think not now on that foolish wench!'

I drew the flower from my breast,
And threw it down beside his feet.
'She lives still, Grandsire, ever will,
Her spirit never will be still,
Till expiation is complete.'

'When I inherit these estates,
I'll bequeath them to Sir Edmund's kin.
Then may her restless spirit rest,
Find peace with others of the blessed,
Her wraith no longer wandering.

Three years passed by, Grandsire long dead,
In vain had I sought Edmund's kin.
Then one strange night of wind and rain,
A maiden to the castle came,
Asked whether she could come within.

Elaine her name, descended from,
That maiden I met in the wood.
I gently drew her in my arms,
Surrendered to her love and charms,
We married as destined we should.

No longer does her namesake roam,
That woodland glade and Bowmere's Lake,
But weekly we that graveside visit,
Place flowers and pray for Edmund's spirit,
Our son now bearing Edmund's name.

GREY WOLF

Pierre Lemaitre was ten years old.
Dark haired and grey of eye,
Deep he grieved his parent's death,
Would miss them until his last breath,
No time remained to weep and sigh.

That plane crash tore his world apart,
As grandfather now sent for him,
His new home far from cities roar,
On Lac Marceau's deep wooded shore
Far jagged ice peaks glistening.

Grandfather was Sioux Indian,
Stern face of creased brown leather,
Years past he built this house of pine,
Where two of them now quiet dine,
Snug from the freezing weather.

Outside the wind howls eerily,
Young Pierre in question lifts his head,
Another sound sweeps through the trees,
Filling him with deep unease,
Eyes narrow now in sudden dread.

'Grandfather, what's that haunting cry,'
'Wolves, my child, it is their call,
Thus they speak unto each other,
Father wolf to young wolf brother,
Hear how their voices rise and fall.'

The months sped by, spring in the air,
Snow has melted all away.
His grandfather looks on in pride,
Pierre now tracking at his side,
A cougar springs, brings down its prey.

They wander on through forest floor,
Two bear cubs scamper down a tree.
Pierre stares on in sheer delight,
The growling cubs roll, squeak and fight,
When grandfather their mother sees.

His hand restrains the boys advance,
Pierre stands still, rigid with fear,
The brown bear towers, stares around,
Drops to all fours upon the ground,
No danger to her small cubs here.

They watch the beaver's build their dam,
As baby otters dive and play,
And down across the turquoise lake,
An eagle swoops, her prey to take,
Struggling fish carries away.

They hear the haunting cry of loon,
See the moose stooping to drink,
The days and weeks speed quickly by,
Pierre now understanding why,
Of the city he now rarely thinks.

Grandfather smokes a special pipe,
Sometimes sleeps the day away.
Pierre starts wandering on his own,
As playful autumn winds make moan,
Dry leaves in brilliant copper sway.

Still at night the wolves he hears,
By their howling strangely drawn,
Practices their mournful keening,
In his mind discerns their meaning,
Waits until sky is flushed with dawn.

He leaves the house above the shore,
Feet bearing him between the trees,
Wanders on, then stands transfixed,
Their eyes upon him coldly fixed,
A pack of snarling wolves he sees.

He stands, puts back his head and howls,
With a wild and wolf like moan,
Then slowly, slowly they advance,
Spring, leap around in playful dance,
Accepting him now as their own.

They disappear now, all but one
Panting, ears pricked, eyes bright,
Who crouches, then leaps away,
Plainly invites the boy to play,
Then hiding, vanishing from sight.

All day and long into the night,

They run and dance together,

Until exhausted, panting lie,

As huge pale moon climbs up on high,

Then rise and leave each other.

Grandfather stood with folded arms,

Waiting for him at the door,

Face calm as he surveys Pierre,

The boy returns him stare for stare,

Please understand, grey eyes implore.

Grandfather nodding to the boy,

No stern look upon him bending,

Instead a smile lights up his face,

Catches him up in proud embrace,

'So, you comprehend life's meaning.'

All creatures brothers are to man,

And we forget this to our shame,

Grandson I think it time you know,

Amongst the Sioux so long ago,

Chief Grey Wolf it was my name.

A grey wolf howled outside that night,

To that call Pierre replies,

Then snuggled down into his bed,

Mysterious dreams flow through his head,

Grey Wolf beside him smiling lies.

THE BALLET SHOES

The album lay upon her lap,
Its contents spanned her eighty years,
She mused upon one faded print,
Brushed aside unbidden tears.

Had that been her, that winsome child,
Curtseying in ballet's pose,
Steps as light as thistledown,
Froth of white on dainty toes.

Ah yes, such was her early dream,
A dancer's future to embrace,
Her jade green eyes so bright with hope,
Until she saw her father's face.

Mother pleaded, dared to entreat,
Her husband stared in ice cold rage,
No child of mine disgrace our name,
Disport herself upon the stage.

She did not marry, had not dared,
To trust her life to any man,
Who might obstruct new chosen path,
Professor's gown fulfilled her plan.

Now long retired, she lived at peace,
A cottage in a woodland glade,
Nor ever thought back to the time,
When ballet's plans were fondly made.

Tonight she heard it yet again,
That desolate cry piercing her heart,
Rose from her bed, slipped on her shoes,
Once more her lonely quest to start.

She walked along a shadowed path,
Where muted bluebells damply bend,
Pale primrose fans spread fairy gold,
As onwards still her footsteps wend.

This darkling track, where does it lead,
Twixt ghostly trunks of silvered birch
And twisted alder, brambles clutch,
She wanders on in troubled search.

An answer knows she must discern,
To this her nightly dreaming quest,
That child, her wistful voice imploring,
Soft sobbing cry affords no rest.

Some weeks ago she heard it first,
Disturbing night's orphic repose,
Bewildered thrust off shards of sleep,
Unwilling from her bed arose.

She lived alone, some child perhaps
Had stolen in from out the dark.
But how, all doors and windows locked,
Yet dog utters protesting bark.

She quietened Wallace, stroked his head,
Unbolted door and stepped outside.
A half hooped moon lent gentle light,
Ragged cloud shapes past it glide.

The cries no longer filled her ears,
Were they a dream, she looked around,
The garden hid no childish form,
A careful search no answer found

Stiff limbs restored her to her bed,
To twist and turn 'til mornings light,
For many weeks those cries disturbed,
But of the child no single sight.

Tonight, she leaned hard on her cane,
And gasped, for there in moonlit glade,
Danced a child in purest white,
With soft fair hair and eyes of jade.

She spun and danced and pirouetted,
On slender, dainty slippered feet,
Twirled and swayed and dipped and leapt,
As winking stars she would entreat.

Mysterious music softly steals,
Upon cold midnights mist damp air,
The child is happy, laughing now,
Completely vanished all despair.

'Who are you, dancing so tonight?'
She softly asks this phantom maid,
The dancer stands in musing pose,
Her pointing fingers gesture made.

The woman stares, for now at last,
She understands those midnight cries,
That had prevented recent sleep,
Regards the child in shocked surprise.

'You tell me, that we two are one,
My childhood's dream once harsh denied,
Unfettered now by time and space,
Here in this moonlight realised.'

She laughs, tosses aside her cane,
Feet bare, she raises hands on high,
Then twirls and leaps in purest joy,
That none may ever now deny.

Eyes closed in death, on lips a smile,
They found her so the following day,
Close beside her in that woodland glade,
A child's white ballet slippers lay.

THE FLOOD

Sun was masked by swarming clouds,
A storm about to break,
The river stroked by eerie light,
Foam crested waves an awesome sight,
The driver must decision make.

Should he turn back, make for home,
Stares uneasy at that sky,
The village just two miles away,
Accelerates, speeds on his way,
Wife utters an impatient sigh.

Look at those clouds, going to pour,
She pats her carefully permed hair,
They've planned this anniversary,
In a Cornish village by the sea,
Place beautiful beyond compare.

A lightning flash now cleaves the sky,
Thunder growls, rain sleeting down,
Windscreen wipers try in vain,
Competing with the lashing rain,
John Masters skids and then slows down.

Hugging that narrow country road,
The river sweeps towards the sea,
John resolutely drives ahead,
The swollen river in its bed,
Now rising fast, he does not see.

At the bottom of the hill,
The village comes in sight at last,
A humpty bridge of ancient stone,
Spans the river's angry moan,
The car approaches—die is cast.

Within the white walled Rose Hotel,
The landlord frowns and shakes his head,
This storm will keep his trade away,
Seems to have set in for the day,
Will cause them many an empty bed.

Stares from the window, face appalled,
Sees wall of water rising high,
Across the bridge sweeps mighty flood,
Fear grips his soul, freezing his blood,
Those in that silver car must die.

The car is tossed like fragile toy,
Bridge crumbles with indignant roar,
Towards the village water races,
Folk with stark fear upon their faces,
Rush inside the nearest door.

John Masters fights unconsciousness,
Surrounded by the water's gloom.
Struggles to release the door,
To his wife swiftly implores,
Make haste, or else this car our tomb.

His body shocked by water's cold,
Now pulls his wife out at his side,
The car swept onwards to the sea,
They surface, gasping, as a tree
Is swept towards them on the tide.

John grabs a branch and holds on tight,
Beside him Mary in despair,
Clutches his legs, raises her head,
Fears that soon she will be dead,
Takes fearful gasps of salty air.

Water still rising, power immense,
Floods across a grassy field,
Sweeps on, its force at last receding,
John gasps in pain, his hands are bleeding,
To shock and cold his body yields.

Mary with unsuspected strength,
Struggles to pull him to dry ground,
Coughing and spluttering both now lie,
On heather bank, hear gulls harsh cry,
John rises, slowly looks around.

They hug each other, both are shaking,
Scarce can believe they are alive,
A lightning flash lights up the sky,
Shines on that water rushing by,
A miracle they have survived.

They must find shelter, look around,
The sky dark as approaching night,
Still the thunder rumbles on,
Their clothes are torn, their shoes are gone,
Utter a prayer so dire their plight.

Then clear upon the Cornish air,
A bell rings out in solemn chime,
John listens, rising to his feet,
Seeking its source, that bell so sweet,
They see the church, towards it climb.

High upon a heathery hill,
It stands against the rain filled sky,
Its windows shining radiant bright,
Blazing out its welcoming light,
To reach it now they desperate try.

The door is heavy, solid oak,
John knocks and calls with urgent voice,
Door slowly opens and a hand,
Beckons them in mute command,
Bell ringing with unearthly noise.

Upon the altar candles blaze,
Walk to the pews and drop in prayer,
Then John and Mary raise their eyes,
Stare at that priest in quiet surprise,
That he keeps lonely vigil there.

His face they see is gentle, kind,
Dark quiet eyes, white beard and hair,
His white robe in the candlelight,
Touched with gold, shimmering bright,
Mary and John, you're welcome here.

He points to their bleeding hands and feet,
Kneels before them, bathes with care,
Then applies a healing balm,
Talks with them voice soft and calm,
Places his hand upon their hair.

His blessing now given, smiles and turns,
Removes his flowing robe and cape,
John and Mary feel sleep stealing,
While still above the bell is pealing,
His robes about them softly drape.

Morning breaks, they stir and wake,
With troubled eyes about them stare,
Above their heads blue open sky,
A ruined church around them lies,
Empty windows, altar bare.

About their shoulders realise,
A length of sacking warmly lay,
Examine once hurt feet and hands,
Completely healed, can't understand,
Bewildered, lower heads and pray.

The massive door stands half ajar,
Hear the plaintive bleat of sheep,
Rise to their feet and step outside,
The flood in which they nearly died,
Has drained back to the river deep.

A shepherd watches in surprise,
What are you two doing here?
The words fall tumbling from their lips,
The flood, the bell, that night worship,
That gentle priest with snow white hair.

Twas old St Aiden that you saw,
For many centuries he's been dead,
They say he comes at times of need,
When help from God his children plead,
Old church transformed, so it is said.

We've heard tales of a phantom bell,
Chiming to warn of storms at sea,
You're greatly blessed, the shepherd said,
Looks at the church in sudden dread,
Come you away now, follow me.

So that was yours, the silver car,
I saw it floating out to sea,
All thought the passengers had died,
Those in the village be surprised,
Goods news at least, your safety be.

What happened to the village, friend,
He told them then in quiet tones,
Many properties destroyed,
The villagers were now employed,
In salvaging their damaged homes.

What will they do, just move away,
By no means, no, they'll start again,
Each hundred years say history's pages,
A tidal surge along river rages,
Bell warning rings, to beasts and men.

Let's go back inside, see the bell,
The shepherd lifts restraining hand,
No bell remains, he said head shaking,
Long years ago they say 'twas taken,
Now phantom bell within God's plan.

The shepherd takes them to his cottage,
Feeds them, phones for help to come,
In a hired car they drive away,
With wonder face another day,
 Anniversary—a memorable one.

GREEK ISLAND

Words--swirling through his head
From deep recesses of his brain.
'Up—up unto the sacred place,
There to receive a special grace'
All morning long heard that refrain.

Left shaggy goats grazing below,
Leapt up the track with lithesome grace,
Paused at entrance to the cave,
Candle lit, expression grave
Entered into that sacred place.

The boy was thin, dark dreaming eyes,
Thick curls black as the ravens wing,
Kneels down on chapels rocky floor,
Voice murmuring—'Lord I thee adore'
Prayed he might hear the angels sing.

Above his head a wondrous scene,
A painting on that ancient wall,
Three figures robed in flowing white,
Upon their heads gleam haloes bright,
Names, none could ever now recall.

The central Saint—Peter perhaps,
Dark bearded face in candles flame
Looked stern, yet eyes were wide with awe,
Some precious vision doubtless saw,
The boy whispered the Saviour's name.

That birth night of the Sacred Child,
Adored by Heaven's wondrous choir,
And of shepherds his old priest had told,
Magi with frankincense, myrrh, gold,
All setting Myron's heart on fire.

He prayed that he one day might hear,
Those mighty wing'ed angels sing,
The candle spluttered, shivered, died,
Dense, thick dark that vault surprised,
Yet to the prayer his lips still cling.

For hours remained there on his knees,
On inner vision still perceived,
Saint's stern face, hands crossed on breast,
But now a smile his mouth caressed,
As though a blessing he now breathed.

Nought broke the silence in that cave
Save the boy's soft whispering prayer,
Then brilliant rainbow light appears,
Radiance so bright, he blinks in fear,
To look around can barely dare.

Then music, such as ears ne'er heard,
Now fill his wondering heart and mind,
Mighty forms, frosted with fire,
Celestial melodies inspire
His soul—to all else he is blind.

He feels rush of departing wings,
As slowly now the radiance fades,
Still in his head that music hears,
Knows it will never disappear,
Strange purpose on his shoulders laid.

He groped his way out on the hill,
Bright sunlight bathed the Isle with gold,
Green wavelets splash the rocky shore,
The herd of goats, his daily chore,
Bleat welcome, Myron to behold.

The priest surveyed him in surprise,
In short black curls two streaks of white,
He speaks no word, as feet advance
Within the church, Priest looks askance,
Follows, listens in awed delight.

Before the organ Myron sits.
Amazing chords his hands caress,
The priest falls down upon one knee,
Glorious, transcendent this melody,
He prays the Lord, Myron to bless.

What miracle untutored lad,
Displays such gift beyond compare,
Mysteriously the music swells,
The priest immobile neath its spell,
The boys own gaze fixed upon the air.

The priest crosses himself in awe,
To the altar rail he clings,
'Where learned such beauteous music, child?'
Myron rose, genuflected--smiled.
'Father, I heard the angels sing.'

POPPY IN THE CORN

The four men bent in unison,
Worked within that field of gold,
Golden corn, a blazing sun,
And yellow tractor, engine old.

Gold on each man's dark brown shirt,
Circle large and yellow bright,
One man paused, his hand was hurt,
The others glad of this respite.

The girl was thin, with soft grey eyes,
She danced between the stooks of corn,
Observed the men in quick surprise,
Youthful interest instant born.

The farmer's youngest daughter she,
They stretched, gave her answering smile,
Each thought of his own family,
Across so many a hundred mile.

Far from Italia's distant shores,
Prisoners now of battle's fate,
Safe from fresh horrors of the war,
Their freedom they can only wait.

Her dress was scarlet, poppy red,
She danced about them like a flame,
Stared at one swarthy face and said,
You've hurt your hand, what is your name.

'Bruno' he gave uncertain glare,
'Mine is Kate' was her reply,
'That circle on the shirt you wear,
Bruno, tell me the reason why?'

'I wear it not myself to please,
Of prisoner of war it is the sign,
My home is far across the seas,
Not here amongst you English swine'.

A fellow prisoner shook his head,
She is but a little girl, amico,
So be polite,' then smiled and said,
'Kate, my name it is Vincento.'

'And and I Ricardo, I am Carlo,
The others introduction made,
But Kate was staring hard at Bruno,
On bleeding hand her kerchief laid.

'Just you wash that cut tonight.'
She tied a knot then stepped away.
Around her golden hair, the light
Shimmered in the heat of day.

The uncut corn with poppies swayed,
Red stars amongst that field of gold,
And poppy bright this little maid,
Bruno's glance did firmly hold.

Examined him, black curls, dark eyes,
A handsome face, but bitter mouth.
A pain his face could not disguise,
A longing to return home south.

Child and man exchanged that look,
Bond was formed that would not break,
Over the months in shady nook,
Shared dreams, a future path to take.

When this war is over,' he would say
I return then to my family farm,
Near sunny Naples, above the bay.'
'If you visit you'll be safe from harm.'

The farmer felt a strong unease,
At Kate's strange friendship with the man,
As stubbled field and russet trees,
Gave way to winters icy plan.

The prisoners now set other tasks,
Repairing wagons, feeding sheep,
Young Kate and Bruno vainly ask,
Permission sometimes still to meet.

'The Italians soon are going home,
Good riddance too,' the farmer said.
'So keep away Kate, nor yet roam,
To meet them in the milking shed.'

Then one sad day of cloud and rain,
A lorry came, the four departed,
No warning, no time to explain,
When Kate heard she was broken hearted.

Six years passed by on restless wings,
Bruno was working in his fields,
He raised his voice, began to sing,
The corn should offer a good yield.

Then paused and stared at one who came,
Across the field between the stooks,
Light her step, dress bright as flame.
She saw him cast ecstatic look.

'Kate—little Kate, can that be you,'
Bruno now called in glad surprise.
She smiled, he saw that it was true,
And stared into her soft grey eyes.

'Carissima, my little Kate,'
He laughed and caught her to his breast.
'I'm eighteen now, just could not wait'
To come to Naples as your guest'

Poppies bled into the corn,
Scarlet as blood no longer shed,
An end to war's virulent storm,
No more fighting, hatred dead.

Now Kate and Bruno work together,

Married, fulfilled, happy and free.

And scarlet poppies bloom forever,

On into eternity.

JUANITA

It was a night of glittering stars,
A soft wind poured from off the sea,
The little waves made murmuring splash,
Dark pines and palms sway over me.
I glance around, restless, concerned,
The girl I love, where can she be.

A half hooped moon, luminous, pale,
Casts silvered net on swelling tide.
White villas beckon on the shore,
But where's the girl I'd make my bride.
A gypsy girl, passionate, proud.
Her promise she had given me.

I hear a laugh, I turn and stare,
And there along moon dappled sand,
Juanita runs, barefoot and free,
Her sandals dangling from one hand.
I rise, then freeze, another man,
Calls to the girl so dear to me.

She stops and opens wide her arms,
He clasps her fast, twirls her around,
And then they kiss, stand breast to breast,
His sombrero falls onto the ground.
'Juanita' now I hear him say,
'You said you'd spend tonight with me'

She hesitates, then shrugs and laughs,
'I know a place within the wood,'
I crouch and watch them climb the bank,
Should I confront them, what's the good.
My gypsy sweetheart, mine no more,
My dream of love—just fantasy.

I walked the shore till it was dawn,
The sun peach bright rose o'er the sea,
Gulls screamed, a coastguard sauntered by,
Then they returned—and stared at me.
She smiled, he nodded, cool, aloof,
Then they walked off beside the sea.

My villa welcomed marble bright,
In courtyard the small fountain played,
On walls the bougainvillea swarmed,
House keeper called, 'Fresh coffee made.'
'You had a good night then Senor,'
Glanced at my face in sympathy.

'That gypsy, she no good, Senor,
She breaks the hearts of all she meet.'
I thanked her, set my easel up,
My fevered brush drops at my feet,
The canvas glowed with subtle charm,
Juanita smiles for all to see.

They hung it in a gallery,
Jaded critics pose and stare.
'The artist's really captured her,
That passionate face, her flowing hair.
Do you think the artist slept with her?'
'Well just look at it—undoubtedly.'

THE MISSING BRIDE

A cool wind brushes o'er his face,
Sweeping from snow peaks above,
Night wears a robe of spangled lace,
As Robert sets out to meet his love.

Along the loch, oars creak and bend,
Lifting with the softest splash,
His two companions do not speak,
Know this adventure truly rash

Castle lights beckon them on,
Within its towers his lady waits,
Laird Broderick he has no son,
His heir therefore is daughter Kate.

A grand marriage now arranged,
Between Kate and his friend MacDuff,
She first refused, must be deranged,
Of protestations he had enough.

Tonight he holds a splendid feast,
At which the marriage will take place,
He hopes some gratitude at least,
A pleasing smile upon her face.

MacDuff might be of portly build,
His hair receding, slightly grey,
But much good would this union yield,
Two great estates conjoined today.

He knocks upon her chamber door,
Her waiting women move aside,
Restrains his preparatory roar,
Kate stands veiled, a lovely bride.

Laird Broderick smiles satisfaction,
Of course he knew she would consent,
That white gown fitting to perfection,
A fond glance now upon her bent.

Mistress, complete your preparation,
Within an hour you will be wed,
Dismiss wilful infatuation,
Make ready to be wife instead.

Present your husband with fine sons,
With smiling lips come to his arms,
And while the sands of life shall run,
He will be faithful to your charms.

She answered not, head averted,
He hesitated, shrugged, could not wait,
Would be furiously disconcerted,
Beneath that veil, it was not Kate.

His daughter on a rope descending,
From turret chamber just below,
Her young life to fate surrendering,
Rope too short, she now lets go.

Into her lover's waiting arms,
Kate gasps, ribs bruised from her fall,
'Quiet mo chridhe, sweet Kate be calm,
Now quick, away from castle wall.'

Kind hands help them in the boat,
As back across the loch it skims,
He shouts from glad exultant throat,
On shore fine horses waiting him.

They gallop off beneath the stars,
To safety of the highland hills,
No pursuit sounding in their ears,
Just night bird's cry and babbling rill.

Back within Kate's bedchamber,
Loyal young maid swiftly disrobes,
Moving fast, that none may blame her,
Throws aside the bridal robes.

Finery swift taken from her hands,
White gown and fine lace veil,
Thrown away as had been planned,
Deep down into a disused well.

The rope by which Kate made escape,
No longer dangles from the wall,
Her aunt hides it beneath her cape,
Revellers gather in the hall.

Kate's attendants now descend,
The laird sees them with content,
Says MacDuff, 'Your daughter's ready friend,
Some hours of waiting we've spent.'

'Your mistress, wenches, where is she.'
'We left her praying on her knees,
Asked that we give her privacy,
She prays her future lord to please.'

'Of her nonsense I've now enough.'
Laird Broderick swift ascends the stair,
Followed by his friend MacDuff,
Find chamber empty, Kate not there.

They stare round in bewilderment,
The chamber had no other door,
Yet she their plans did circumvent,
Laird Broderick lets out a roar.

Women now questioned, show no fear,
Answer with great innocence,
Twas the fairies made her disappear,
Broderick howls in impotence.

Within the hills, a hidden cave,
Here Kate and Robert now are wed,
The priest his gentle blessing gave,
Wishing them joy at board and bed.

No bridal veil of whitest lace,
No future life of luxury,
But firelights gleam adorns her grace,
As Robert her true beauty sees.

They sleep upon a heather couch,
Embrace neath Robert's woollen plaid.
While Broderick and MacDuff slouch
Drunken to bed, enraged and sad.

A legend grew about that night,
The lass the fairies stole away,
Complete with wedding gown so white,
The tale continues so today.

THE MOOR

Wind scoured shivering heather slopes
With cold, ferocious breath.
Grey scudding cloud obscured the sun,
As Robbie raised his father's gun,
Reverberating across the heath.

The rabbit, yes, he'd brought it down,
His dog swift to retrieve it.
It lay with sad and glazing eyes,
As death its agile form surprised,
The lad could scarce believe it.

His father would be proud of him,
Yet no doubt would swear and scold.
He took the gun without consent,
Away across the moorland went,
Out on this day of wind and cold.

Brogues were wet, knees scratched by gorse,
Ears pierced by peewit's plaintive cry.
He bent above the furry shape,
That his swift shot could not escape,
One final leap, to fall and die.

As he stared down, a darting thought
Assailed his young and careless mind.
That life so sudden could depart,
Compassion softly touched his heart,
The rabbit's sight to life now blind.

And as he stood there all alone,
He rubbed his unbelieving eyes.
Around him all was realigned,
Place unfamiliar, ill defined,
As shouts and groans in chorus rise.

All about him men lie dead,
Or wounded in their final throes,
Marching away across the heath,
Where they'd exacted fearsome death,
A red coat troop exultant go.

'Water—of your mercy lad,'
He heard the clansman's feeble cry.
The tartan plaid bore deepening stain,
The man's blue eyes, red rimmed with pain,
Bleeding from chest, exposed thigh.

A swift wee burn gurgled close by,
Robbie bent and cupped his hands,
Water touched the man's parched lips,
He raised his head, took further sips,
As Robbie tried to understand.

What was happening on this moor,
Where shattered forms lay in their pain.
'Did the bonnie Prince get safe away,'
He heard the wounded clansman say.
Was this was the '45' again.

'However long a time it takes
Scotland will rise, be free again.'
Robbie heard final rattling breath,
The blue eyes glazed and closed in death,
An end now to the clansman's pain

The boy fell down upon his knees,
Stroked the clansman's bloodstained brow,
Then as he knelt, a change took place,
Instead of clansman's youthful face,
A brown furred rabbit lay there now.

His hand a rabbit gently stroked,
Bewildered snatched his hand away.
What strange and curious trick of time,
Had played just now in ancient mime,
The shock on his emotions played.

He rose and left the rabbit there,
Shouldered the gun, no more to fire.
Blundered back upon the moor,
Then stopped by Tom the Shepherd's door,
'Come in lad, sit ye by the fire.'

Tom's wise old eyes surveyed the lad,
To him the story was not strange.
'My son, it seems you have the sight,
On Culloden's moor you saw the fight,
That caused our history sad to change.'

'But the rabbit and the dying man,
From this what meaning should I sift?'
The old man nodded silver head,
'Well, both of them were lying dead,
Life is God's most precious gift.'

'Men need to learn to live together,
For animals show respect and care.
Before their blood we wanton spill,
Ask is it right to maim and kill,
From wars try always to forebear.

Yet freedom is a mighty flame,
That leaps up in the heart of man,
Nothing can its passion dim,
Deep in our souls its sacred hymn,
Injustice still its embers fan.

So these two thoughts combine together,
From violence draw back aside,
Freedom lives within man's heart,
A vote can free him now to start,
New road with dignity and pride.

Then Robbie tramped on through the heather,
Perhaps with more maturity.
The wind had dropped, clouds had scattered,
Sun broke through and all that mattered,
He would be back in time for tea.

THE GREAT GLEN

Oh have ye seen the great glen,
When evenings shadows fall,
Deep pulsing red of brooding cloud,
And mist to wrap the land in shroud,
Of mystic beauty, that enthrals.

Oh have ye glimpsed the antlered stag,
Looming wraith like on the moor,
To vanish onto heathered height,
As sinking orb spills splintered light,
Down sombre flanks of dark Ben More.

Oh have ye heard the eagle's cry,
Swooping from high peaks above,
As gurgling, deep burns darkling flow,
Neath brackened banks, in twilights glow
Earth's murmured rhapsody of love.

Oh have ye seen dark storm clouds lour,
Bursting black fury on the hill,
Breathed pungent fragrance of crushed heather,
Rain-swept yet joying in the weather,
Plunged onwards, long dreams to fulfil.

Have ye walked a moonlit path,
Snaking through a haunted glen,
Where battle cries from men of yore,
Rise from an earth once drenched in gore,
Warrior blood of Highland men.

And have ye seen fair light of dawn,
Flood golden, sweeping from the Ben,
Whilst on fragile bluebells fairies play,
As purple foxgloves dip and sway,
And bird song sweetens all the glen.

And hast seen lace of waterfalls,
Glittering after shower of rain,
Dark clouds pale rimmed with silver light,
As timid sheep now turn in fright,
And forwards you advance again.

All this remains on memory's page,
Shining sea lochs, gulls harsh cry,
Bell heather red in sinking sun,
Those phantom deer when day is done,
All in my heart, until I die.

JUNGLE RESCUE

The pit they dug was ten feet deep,
They covered it with branches green,
Laughed and left, to eat and sleep,
Nor knew their actions had been seen.

He stood and shuddered with unease,
From swaying trunk, to small bright eyes,
Watched them steal off between the trees,
Those man creatures that he despised.

The young bull hidden from their sight,
Within the jungle's dappled shade,
Watched long into the starlit night,
Felt curious, but not afraid.

Why had the men dug that pit,
Then to the river bank drawn back,
His busy mind considered it,
As he watched heard gentle crack.

A young gazelle leapt in the glade,
Pursued by leopard fierce and fleet,
The deer a mighty effort made,
Cleared the pit on flying feet.

The leopard in pursuit now falls,
Imprisoned in that pit below,
With fright and anger screaming calls,
Gazelle in panic onwards goes.

The leopard makes repeated leap,
Vain attempting to win free,
Alas the pits sides are too steep,
Prowls, back and forth despairingly.

Above the pit grey monkeys chatter,
Laugh at the leopard's sorry plight,
Around the edge with quiet patter,
Hyena sneaks, eyes evil, bright.

Alone in all that jungle deep,
The elephant shows no disdain,
But still his lonely vigil keeps,
Considering the leopard's pain.

Then within its busy brain,
The great beast makes a careful plan,
The answer to the problem plain,
To thwart the cruelty of man.

Thrashed around in hurried search,
Seized massive bough of fallen tree,
Turning now with backward lurch,
The leopard very soon be free.

With careful trunk lowers the bough,
Inside that pit ladder provides,
The leopard watches knowing now,
It can escape the pits steep sides.

Its green eyes with unwinking glare,
Survey this friend out of the night,
Climbs up and out, crouches and stares,
Makes growling purr, springs out of sight.

The elephant trumpets in delight,
Removes pits leafy camouflage,
No other friends suffer this plight,
Then lurches off in boisterous charge.

Morning dawns, the men return,
Stare at the pit in baffled rage.
Eyes in sheer frustration burn,
No trophies to put in their cage.

Wonder as they see that bough,
Sides deep scratched by leopard's claws,
Uneasily demanding how,
Someone dared its vicious jaws.

And who removed green covering,
Their clever jungle trap exposed,
Some foe perhaps is hovering,
Rival trappers they supposed.

And yet no footprints but their own,
The deep and empty pit surround,
Some genie of the night had flown,
To haunt this stretch of ravaged ground.

The great bull trumpets eerily,
Voice joined by leopard's throaty cough,
They turn in fear, run speedily,
Of this adventure they'd enough.

Much money they are always paid,
For the beasts they frequent trap,
To this particular leafy glade,
Resolve they never will come back.

THE BRIDGE

An old stone bridge spanned the stream,
No more than three yards wide.
Beneath it water gurgles slow,
The woman leans to watch its flow,
Thoughts borne on memories tide.

As child she'd clambered down this bank,
Empty jam jar on the sand.
The tiny minnows caught in play
Releases, sees them swim away,
Her fishing net trails in her hand.

She looks across the meadow,
Does it flood still in spring-----
Wading water shallow, cold,
Where kingcups thrust in clumps of gold,
Sun on the water glittering.

She sighed and memory faded,
Replaced now by another.
A young girl sitting on the bridge,
A nightingale sang in the hedge,
As she waited for her lover.

Sunset was fading into dusk.
Lips met in passionate kiss.
They wandered to a secret place,
Safe to share love's fond embrace,
All too short the lovers bliss.

A world war took her love away,
Metal wings soared in the sky.
Opponents dive in deadly game,
Spitfire explodes, falls down in flames,
A telegram---why did he die.

She never married after that,
Became a nurse, made it her life.
Now silver haired she has retired,
To recall childhood now inspired,
This nursing sister, but no wife.

'It's hot today,' she lifts her head,
The stranger looks at her and smiles
'Bill Roberts, it's my farm you know,
Saw you a few times, long ago,'
His face was honest, without guile.

'It was at the village dance,' he said,
'During the war, when we were young.
I ran the farm, so did not fight,
At the time didn't feel quite right,
But the crops helped our country run'

Those bright blue eyes and bushy brow,
She looked at him, remembering how.
He'd bent and asked if she would dance,
But deep in love, bound by romance,
Declined, saw his departing bow.

The news had come of Richard's death,
She'd left the village, moved away,
As student nurse had then enrolled,
To men's advance remote and cold,
His memory she could not betray.

Yet here upon this old stone bridge,
She stared at one from out the past,
Like hers his hair was silver now,
His smile the same, his bushy brow,
She turned her head away at last.

'Mary, you stole my heart you know,'
He gently said and took her hand.
No ring it bore, she was not wed,
'I am a nurse,' she firmly said,
'Bill Roberts, please let go my hand.'

'Only if you will promise make,
That we may meet, just tell me when.'
Their eyes met, brown stared into blue.
She slowly nodded, knew it true,
The bridge had called her back again.

She felt its stones still wondering.
Its water gurgling brown and slow,
 Like this her life had so far been,
But like it's ever moving stream
Fate urged her now to onwards go.

THE HARPIST

The sun low sinking
Leaving trail of indigo and rose.
Driver taking bends too fast,
Shepherd pauses, face aghast,
As speeding on the red car goes.

On into the gathering dusk,
Mist floating down between the hills,
Violet haze masks the stars,
Towards him streaks another car,
Crashes, sits there shaken, still.

The other car disappears,
He screams, tries to force the door,
Smells the petrol, scrambles free,
Runs down the bank, behind a tree,
Explosion shakes him to the core.

Wonders now what place is this.
Back in the flames phone and maps,
The burning car's fierce lurid glow,
No sign of habitation shows,
Curses his concentration's lapse.

Far below the highland road
Waters of a loch gleam gold,
Reflecting the still leaping flames,
The other car now rightly blames,
Starts to shiver from the cold.

Staggers back across the road,
Above him dark dense forest looms.
Hesitates, plunges ahead,
Desperate for help, food, a bed,
Plunges in all enveloping gloom.

Wanders wildly through the trees,
His chest is aching, vision poor,
Then blinks, that light is it a dream,
Walks towards its distant gleam,
Knocks upon the cottage door.

No answer to his urgent knock.
But stealing softly to his ear,
Chords that are a sheer delight,
Stealing mysterious through the night,
Melody rising tender, clear.

Richly sweet the harp vibrates,
Drips melancholy into the night.
Then a woman's voice rose and fell,
He feels loathe to break the spell,
But for the singer longs a sight.

Places eye to that small crack,
Where wooden shutters do not meet.
Slender she was and dark of hair,
He saw her face was very fair,
Her dress long, falling to her feet.

No doubt likes her solitude,
This place so lonely, so remote
From neighbours, shops, so very far,
Yet here she was alone, no car,
And still the music round her floats.

Returning now to the door,
Pushes it open, in he goes,
Inside the kitchens very cold,
Shelves look dusty, cobwebbed, old,
Opened the inner door then froze.

How beautiful the woman was,
From shining hair to deep blue eyes,
Her graceful hands still pluck the strings,
As to the melody she sings,
Nor looks at him, to his surprise.

'Hallo there, lady', he begins,
'I'm truly sorry to intrude,
You see, my car crashed on the road,
Fuel caught, made it explode,
Please listen, don't wish to be rude.'

'Have you a mobile I can use,
I need to contact the police'
But still she sings there soft and low,
He stares bewildered, turns to go,
Heart beating fast with strange unease.

Poignant now the woman's voice,
The music seems to fill his head,
The words she sings foreign, strange,
Gaelic perhaps, amazing range,
He watches her in sudden dread.

Now she sets aside the harp,
Rises tall to dainty feet,
Stares at him, her eyes blue flame,
Softly speaks aloud his name,
'John McGregor, kiss me,' lips entreat.

He turns from her and flees,
Into the dark and whispering night,
Runs blundering back through the trees,
Nor stops until the road he sees,
Eyes are shocked and wide with fright.

By his still smouldering car,
A police car's flashing lights.
With the officers a shepherd stands,
Reaching out with helpful hands,
'Puir laddie, he looks unco white.'

So said the shepherd now,
Watching him with deep concern.
'What did ye in the forest, lad,
By your face saw something awful bad,
We waited here for your return.'

'Now sit you down, sir.'
He swayed as officer's strong grip,
Lowered him down upon the bank,
 As he murmurs quiet thanks,
Through his white and shaking lips.

'Now sir, just tell us your name.'
'John McGregor—Canadian,' he replied.
'Another car drove straight at me,
I know I crashed against a tree,
He drove off, I nearly died.'

'Went off through the trees,
Hoping house and help to find,
In a clearing, cottage all alone,
Music such as I've never known,
Stealing through my heart and mind.'

'Was it then a harpist, lad,
A woman harpist that ye heard,'
So asked the shepherd's urgent tone,
'A woman living on her own,
Voice sweeter, than the sweetest bird.'

'You know of her,'
'Oh yes, I do,' the shepherd said.
'They say that she was black of hair,
Eyes gentian blue, face very fair,
Over two centuries been dead.'

The officers just stand and stare,'
The old man's mind was wandering.
Yet he it was who called them here,
His mobile message very clear,
Exchange their glances, pondering.

'You were perhaps driving too fast.'
'Yes. Brakes failed me way back in the hills,
All I could do was drive straight on.
Until my fuel was all gone,
I was not driving so for thrills.

The shepherd drew a sudden breath,
Of the officers inquired,
'Number of the other car I gave,
That almost sent him to his grave,
To whom is it registered.'

'That information must be withheld,
Not to be given now, my friend.'
'Officer it has much bearing,
On all that we're presently hearing,
I ask you now to unbend.'

'Campbell, Roderick Campbell,'
'It was so I thought that it might be.
John McGregor, just tell me how,
The woman treated you just now,'
'She kissed me very tenderly.'

'She knew my name,
'John McGregor, kiss me,' said.
I drew her close within my arms,
Deep drawn to her grace and charms,
Her lips were ice, I turned in dread.'

'That music of that harp,
Will pursue me throughout life.
Just tell me shepherd, who was she,
The girl whose music s haunting me,
I sensed she'd been caught up in strife.'

'Catriona McGregor she,
Wife to John of that same name,
After the fatal 'Forty-five'
Neither of them left alive,
To the Campbell's bitter shame.'

'Young John took to the hills,
Dared attempt his wife to see,
Within their cottage, that young maid,
Upon her harp sweet music played,
Rippling chords soar wild and free.'

'Across the waters of the loch,
He rowed to her in his small boat,
A Campbell troop they lie in wait,
The eagle returns to his mate,
Him they shoot, then slit her throat.'

'They say her music still,
Is heard by those bearing her name.
Throughout the years, some have seen,
This harpist caught in memories dream.
To have been scared sir, it was no shame.'

An ambulance at last appears,
With whine and lights that flash and blink.
The officers their notes complete,
Each other's eyes, sheepishly meet,
Wondering what will their sergeant think.

The paramedics help him in,
 A few cracked ribs they now decide.
John calls the shepherd, lifts his head,
 'My thanks, what is your name,' he said.
'Why, 'tis McGregor,' the man replied.

THE SNOW MELTS

Ice has cracked, snow melted all
away, as water crystal clear, dripping,
trickling, glittering, swirling—cascading
from the waking hills--rushes in silvered
waterfalls--wildly leaping ancient rocks,
downwards, ever downwards towards
the bright green sea.
Now nature strokes this magic Isle
in gold of pale primrose, buttercups,
blaze of gorse, while stately,
yellow iris line the burn.
Swift dives the playful otter, uttering
joyful squeaks and shrieks,
swimming, streaking, ever seeking
the illusive fish.
Puffins and gilliemot seek purchase
on each ledge and shelf of rock,
above those dizzying heights,
where far below a wild sea boils and
surges, lashing black rocks with high

flung spumes of foam.

Black backed gulls scream, dive, sail the wind,

shouting challenge to leaping

dolphins and minky whale.

Deer leap like drifting ghosts

against the hill, as above all, the

golden eagle soars majestic, supreme,

surveying his kingdom—

All this is Skye, island of my dreams

and long love, treasure house of

memories and other moments

yet unborn.

THE CHOIR

The tourist scanned the brochure,
Listing places to explore,
New gem of interest to glean,
Museum, art galleries now seen,
Mounts steps to the cathedral door.

The vaulted roof above his head,
Fine arches sculpt of ancient stone,
Stained glass and statues wondrous wrought,
He stares at all in careless thought,
Uneasy that he is alone.

Legs are tired, slides in a pew,
Musing with supercilious air,
How strange through centuries of time.
Mislead by myths doubtless sublime,
Man built such edifice to prayer.

He thanks the fates his mind is free,
Of superstition's cloying dream,
Those who believe, well that's their loss,
His eyes light on the golden cross,
Outlined by candles gentle gleam.

Above the altar's linen cloth,
That cross seems to increase in size,
Impossible to shift his gaze,
His eyes unable to abase
Bewildered gasps in shocked surprise.

Shaking now in all his limbs,
Within his mind discerns a voice,
Stern but beautiful the words,
Such as he had never heard,
Presenting him life changing choice.

He lower's head in trembling prayer,
Perceives a truth ne'er glimpsed before,
Feels soothing touch upon his hair,
Dispelling pride and life's despair,
Forgiveness now his lips implore.

Self pride had all channels blocked,
To Christ's redeeming love,
Now stream of Living Waters flow,
God's healing grace gently bestow,
In wondrous blessing from above.

He kneels beneath that soaring vault,
Lips murmuring repentant prayer,
When soft upon his wondering ear,
Hears music stealing rich and clear,
Beauteous chords beyond compare.

Amazed he listens mystified,
That earth's musicians could enthral
The spirit with such magic sound,
Soaring, lilting all around,
Sweet silvered notes now rise and fall.

Theme taken up by sweet voiced choir,
In fervent ecstasy of praise,
Their voices soar in exultation,
Offering Heaven's own oblation,
To be remembered all his days.

No longer knew how long he knelt,
Absorbed in prayer, his joy complete,
As gradually the music ceased,
Bestowing benison of peace,
At last he rises to his feet.

A white haired priest slowly approached,
This lonely worshipper to greet,
Father, that choir I just heard sing,
They made the very Heavens ring,
The world's best singers not compete.

The priest just stared in quick surprise,
A gentle smile enhanced his face,
My son, whilst you knelt there to pray,
No earthly choir sang here today,
Save afforded by our Saviour's grace.

It may be from celestial realms,
This wondrous music filled your soul,
'Tis only when the mind is still,
And we surrender to His will,
Our heavenly Father makes us whole.

Once more out in the busy street,

Joy new discovered fills his mind

God's healing love, before unknown,

His life no longer his alone,

Future beckons, past left behind.

THE CONCERT

I take my seat, knees slightly cramped,
Peer down upon the stage below.
Thoughts of discomfort swift dissemble,
As orchestra starts to assemble
Shining brass, and fevered bow.

They tune up, pour discordant sound
Upon protesting, outraged ears,
Such cruel assault, never cease,
At last oh bliss, island of peace,
Conductor from the wings appears.

Long haired, black coated, debonair,
Receives obligatory applause,
Explains the works so soon to play,
Respect to the composers pays,
Faces his orchestra—a pause.

First work by Bridges is 'The Sea'.
He raises long, expressive hands,
And now with faultless artistry,
Ascends this music of the sea,
Gently slapping on the sand.

I gasp, the sweetness of the sound,
Transports me to a world of dreams,
The strings with tenderness implore,
As flute and horn the theme explore,
Swift wavelets crested by moonbeams.

The sea in all its moods is captured,
Storm with timpanic fury bent,
Waters lift their glistening flanks,
Exposing chasms deep and dank,
The music now slowly relents.
The storm has passed and now the sea,
Shines blue beneath a radiant sun,
Waves with a myriad sequins gleam,
As now relinquishing my dream,
I realise the work is done.

Applause so fully is deserved,
Hundreds of stinging hands agree,
Now to my joyful comprehending,
Vaughn Williams joyful Lark Ascending,
Small harbinger of heavenly glee.

Thready sweetness now uplifting,
Spirits to celestial realm.
The solo violinist's skill
Down my back sends fevered chill,
Conductor's genius at the helm.

That fragile, feathered, flexing throat,
As tiny wings soar swift above,
Pouring sweetness down below,
Praise to its Maker passionate flows,
In melody of purest love.

The orchestra surrounds the theme,
Wraps it about in joyous surge,
Following that ecstatic flight,
In rhapsody of sheer delight,
Music and chorister now merge.

Huge auditorium then resounds
To wave of thunderous acclaim,
Solo violinist now,
Has taken many a graceful bow,
Encore plays of Spanish fame.

The thoughtful interval is over,
Audience return to their seats,
Conductor lifts expressive hands,
Joy of 'The Pastoral' expands,
Horns and strings wistful entreat.

I study the conductor's back
He moves with ballet's matchless grace,
Traditional baton has he none,
But web of beauty golden spun,
As hands the orchestra embrace.

Transported now to woodland dell,
The music soars on magic wings,
Within that woodland forest glade,
Diffusing sun in dappled shade,
Floods joyous brass and vibrant strings.

Memories flood within my mind,
My children's youth, talent so fresh,
Piano, violin and horn,
Drums and guitar, with new life born,
Beauty at last my ears caress.

A son and daughter by my side,
I watch their faces and now see,
Their love which nothing can subdue,
For music's beauty, urgent, true,
Embracing times own melody.

A lullaby of tender notes,
Gently restores attention down,
Beethoven's sunlit 'Pastoral'
To love's emotion softly calls,
This its fragrant, flower decked crown.

Conductor turns a smiling face,
Gracious acknowledges applause,
Back and forth with courteous smile,
Ecstatic audience beguiles,
He leaves we all make for the doors.

That concert remain in my mind,
For many a mundane year ahead,
Music indeed the food of love,
A gift to us from God above,
Without it—soul is truly dead.

The sea, a lark, a woodland glade,
To reappear on memories page,
Music again will play its part,
To warm the lost and aching heart,
Unlock frustrations rigid cage.

*(To my daughter Tania and son Karl
who were present at a memorable concert).*

THE POOL

Here it was, the path
She once had trod----and wandered
in her many dreams!
But was it?
Trees---tall trees bordered it now.
The lane then led twixt
Frothing white of May blossom, and
Cream elderflowers.
Her nostrils sought the illusive scents.
Eyes dropped seeking clumps of bluebells.
No-----well---things change over
fifty years!
Why then she mused, she had
Run---almost danced
To meet him. Now a stick was her
Companion, arthritic pace
Measured, slow.
Now sound of water and
Here it was---the stream!
And just beyond---the pool.

Their pool!

Ah—this had not changed.

Trembling reeds---shimmering winged

Demoiselles----king-cups glowing gold

In the damp green grass.

She knelt---stiffly, painfully

Glanced down into the pool--

Staring at her reflection.

Silver hair---face lined, serene

Eyes a faded blue.

A stickleback rose disturbing the surface,

And the image vanished.

She sighed, about to rise.

Then it happened.

A voice echoing

Back, over the years---a voice

Speaking her name and

Mirrored below her, his

Face! Black hair, dark eyes,

Warm smile and seductive accent

Lent of his Tuscan hills

Bruno whom she had

Loved with the intense passion of

Girlhood.

Beside his face, she

Saw her own, hair auburn

Eyes shining with love.

She felt his kiss upon

Her parted lips.

'Carissima----we must always be

together! When I am no longer

Prisoner of war, we will

Marry---make our home

In Italy'

She had believed him,

Nor understood why he had

Never returned to their meeting place

By the pool.

Then she heard it.

He had been killed. Knocked over

By a passing lorry.

To have survived the war

And died under the wheels

Of a goods lorry!

'Carissima---we will be together

Again---one day----one day!'
The voice ceased---the reflection
Vanished. She rose to
Her feet and smiled.
She must make haste. Her son
Had agreed to drive her to
This place in the village of
Her youth—he and another waiting
In the lay-by for her return.
'Mother----Darling I was getting worried!
You said you would only be about
Ten minutes.'
Well, she thought, at one time it
Would have taken about that.
She stared at him. Stared at her handsome
Middle aged son, with his
Father's dark hair and eyes and
Caressing smile.
'Thank you for taking me back
To a place of my dreams
Of my girlhood,' she said.
Then her husband spoke.
'Get in, Mary. You should

Not go gallivanting off at

Your age!'

Dear, dependable Robert.

Fair hair faded to grey, jovial face

Creased to a smile.

She looked at them with tenderness,

Her husband---and her son

Her son---not his!

ORD OF THE SPRING

Ord of the spring,
Blessed by St Congall,
Water so pure
It sparkles with light.
Drops gently soothing
Life's bruising journey,
Caressed by wild iris
Golden and bright.

Ord of the flowing wave,
Heaven's message bearing,
Lapping small islets
Slapping the shore.
Gulls laughing, screaming,
Small rabbits chasing,
Wind ruffling the wild flowers,
By 'Shore Cottage' door.

Ord of the mountains,
Blaaven your sentinel,
Mysteriously beckoning
Through gossamer mist.
Sgurr Alistair thrusting,
His peak sharply soaring,
Throwing shadow on waters
Of pale amethyst.

Ord of long memories,
Wistfully calling,
Heather hills glowing
As sun sinks to rest,
Rose tinted islands,
Gently fade in the twilight
Sheep plaintively calling,
Ord of the blessed.

CHARLES EDWARD

Charles Edward has a handsome face,
A Stuart Prince, of lineage true
Walks and rides with matchless grace,
Wears powdered wig and coat of blue.

A rapier hanging at his side,
The land with blood he soon will drench,
To Scotland comes in youthful pride,
The throne from German George to wrench.

We love him for his easy charm,
His courage not to be denied,
Mothers, wives feel no alarm
As hundreds gather to his side.

But many more to their deep shame,
Refrain to fight, and yet worse still
Lift swords to back King George's name,
Fellow countrymen to kill.

But most take Charlie to their hearts,
Clans have risen, banners wave,
The cream of Scotland's youth now start,
Their march towards a hero's grave.

But first great victories enjoy,
With song and dancing, spirits high,
Decide which troops they will deploy,
Scotland free or thousands die.

The army seems unstoppable,
English fall back to their advance,
Charles thinks it thing impossible,
That he should be forced back to France.

But men are weary, need to rest,
Now few short miles to London pause,
Should they march on, yet further press,
But these men are tired now of wars.

Charles and his generals decide,
Their future on a turn of card,
The Prince frustrated in his pride
To lose his prize so very hard.

The curse of Scotland, card so called,
They give their orders, turn away,
Charles and his friends are quite appalled,
Their plans should terminate this way.

Unknown the Duke of Cumberland,
Is drawing nearer to the Scots,
His army fresh and better armed,
Mow hundreds down, with musket shot.

Back, back across the border now,
The remnant proudly soldier on,
None will give in firmly avow,
All hope of final victory gone.

Oh for a Wallace or a Bruce,
To lead them in these last few days,
Upon that desolate moor no truce,
On history's page their courage blaze.

Culloden ran red with the blood,
The heart blood of its finest sons,
Twisted they lay, now raven's food,
The moor red as the sinking sun.

Such cruelty was meted out,
By redcoat Army's savagery,
Wounded butchered, no sigh nor shout,
Death of England's chivalry.

To Butcher Cumberland's dismay,
The prize he sought, not his to take,
Charles Edward has got clean away,
Plans for France all he can make.

Redcoat's revenge was very savage,
Burned houses, killing man and beast,
Women and children all are ravaged,
Freedom's dream a sorry feast.

An old man watches as they leave,
With stolen booty heavy laden,
Such cruelty can scarce believe,
His arm supports a weeping maiden.

'Grandfather, will he come again,
The bonny Prince of all our hearts.'
He shook his head, 'I know not when
But can at least safely depart.'

'When will our country then be free
Released from cruel English yoke.'
The old man knelt upon his knee,
His eyes triumphant as he spoke.

Freedom lies within man's heart,
Suffering cannot that passion dim,
Whatever hurt King George impart,
Our people not bow down to him.

Many moons may pass away,
Hard times, oppression bring their pain,
Until at last will dawn the day,
When Scotland shall be free again.

ODE TO BARNABY

I am Barnaby-----Barnaby Cat,
I deign to reside in a Willowbrae flat
With Tania, whom I have patiently trained,
To fulfil all my needs, as I will explain,
For a human she's almost as wise as a cat.

I am Barnaby—forget if you dare,
Disdainful, determined and so debonair,
Will open your fridge with the greatest of ease,
Sleep on your bed, or wherever I please,
Claw your couch or chair with nonchalant air.

I am Barnaby---I do not like shocks,
Such as finding an unwanted visiting fox,
But am partial admit to a tasty small mouse,
Dutifully bring it to share in the house,
Such efforts my mistress distressingly blocks.

I am Barnaby---do whatever I wish,

Stretch up to your plate, swipe your ham or your fish,

Knead your sweater, fall into blissful deep sleep,

Or dance like a banshee with fierce springing leap,

Or devour your yoghurt, my favourite dish.

I am Barnaby—will show I am able,

With wild feline grace to leap onto your table,

Once firmly ensconced will simply not budge,

Until Tania applies an over firm nudge,

Leap down in umbrage, language execrable.

I am Barnaby---will purr to your stroke,

Tolerant when Tania enjoys a quick smoke,

Our secret you see—we respect one another,

Have deep affection one for the other,

For we are both Barnaby—Barnaby folk!

DANCE THE NIGHT AWAY

Dance with me my darling,
Dance the night away,
For I'm off to Afghanistan
At the break of day.

Back to land of burning sand,
Nights of freezing breath,
Where opium poppies gently sway,
Offering oblivion, death.

Mountains tower against the sky,
Suicide bombers roam,
The roads all lined with killer mines,
In a box they send you home.

Then must you go, my darling lad,
Why not stay here with me.
Duty calls and I must fight,
For Queen and my country.

I'll be surrounded by my mates,
We look out for each other,
When you fight, a mate can be,
Closer than a brother.

When rockets streak towards you,
Bullets whine and ricochet,
You fight down fear, just carry on
To fight another day.

But what's this war all about,
My darling, please explain.
What takes you to Afghanistan
With all that fear and pain.

Well, there's women wearing burkas,
Afraid to show their face,
Girls who cannot go to school,
The whole thing a disgrace.

Taliban and Al Quaeda,
We have to drive them back,
Back to their mountain lairs,
Where kalashnikovs still crack.

Sometimes I try to understand,
The real reason why,
Our country is involved this way,
Our troops fight there and die.

Perhaps the politicians,
On both sides of the war,
Will sort out the rights and wrongs,
So we may fight no more.

But until then my darling,
Let's dance the night away,
For I'm off to Afghanistan,
At the break of day.

ABENA

Wandering around the craft fair,
There was so much to see,
A noisy crowd about her hums,
Seeking saris, kaftans, bongo drums,
She stares at handmade pottery.

Pauses by embroidered cushions,
Mexican perhaps could be,
Their sequins glitter in the light,
Boleros too in colours bright,
On next stall Kenyan jewellery.

All handcrafted beads, she hears,
Loves their feel, their earthy shades,
Restlessly she wanders on,
Necklace now her throat adorns,
Under hot sunlight had been made.

Pauses, at stall of wooden crafts,
Giraffes, hippos, elephant,
Dainty gazelles, and then she gasps,
The price she hardly dares to ask,
Wide eyed drawn to the statuette.

The stall holder observing her,
Sees the wonder in her eyes,
He lifts the carving in his hands,
Her love for it quite understands,
Such longing causes no surprise.

He'd watched her wandering about,
Something set this girl apart,
Lifting his dark, Ghanaian head,
'You like this carving,' softly said?
Senses the tumult in her heart.

Flashing knowing wide, white smile,
'Lady, I think you like Abena,'
'Is that her name,' she lightly asks
To chat with her no doubt his task,
This carving—wished she hadn't seen her

She couldn't take her eyes away,
Some two foot tall the figure stood,
'Excuse me, but where was she made,'
'The Gambia where sometimes I trade,
 This is ebony a costly wood.'

'But to be honest with you now,
A Kenyan made her decoration,
This thin gold wire about her neck,
Her skirt, ear-rings and small anklet,
The artist needs much commendation.'

'Oh yes, I totally agree.
But in the Gambia she was made?'
She reaches out with eager touch,
'The price, just tell me now how much?'
'What do you offer me,' he said.

'She's probably beyond my reach,
I am not rich,' the woman sighs.
He stares into her eyes of blue,
Wide, earnest eyes, expression true,
'Well—twenty pounds,' he now replies.

Opening her purse she looks,
One such note she still possessed,
'She's worth much more than that I think,'
Her words almost made him blink,
Rightly this woman he'd assessed.

'Lady—you should take her,'
His words were quiet, firmly spoken,
Maria eyes the figurine,
The loveliest thing she'd ever seen,
The price he asks the merest token.

'Yes, I'll buy her willingly,
But hope the price you will not rue.'
'I'm glad Abena goes to one,
Who one day may feel the Gambia's sun
For Africa is calling you.'

'My name it is Kofi Tchembe,
I hope one day we meet again.'
He carefully wraps Abena up,
Swathed about in bubble wrap,
She smiles, walks out into the rain.

Gets off the bus, finds her key,
Relaxes, kicking off her shoes.
Then unwraps the statuette,
Looks with bated indrawn breath,
Right position must careful choose.

For now stands her upon the table,
While welcome cup of coffee sips,
Figurine's hands crossed on her breast,
One knee is bent beneath her dress,
Face brooding, with full pouting lips.

'You are extraordinary,' she sighs,
'I wonder who modelled this for you.
Such barbaric elegance portrayed,
The carver by your beauty swayed,
Was he perhaps in love with you?'

She sat there dreaming in her chair,
Closed eyes drifting into sleep......
Finds herself in forest glade,
And there beneath its dappled shade,
A youth and girl assignment keep.

Skins are dark and velvet black,
The man is tall, handsome and bold,
The girl so graceful, very shy,
Full pouting lips and wide dark eyes,
The couple hands tenderly hold.

The sleeper murmurs in her chair,
'It is Abena that I see.'
The couple now closely embrace,
When suddenly towards them race
Fierce men, spears levelled angrily.

'My daughter, she is not for you,'
So speaks their Chief with silver hair,
The girl he now attempts to seize,
She turns to run between the trees,
To lovers hand clings in despair.

Together run to river bank,
He plunges in, she at his side,
Furious shouts, spears whistle down,
Current so strong, she fears to drown,
Kwame encourages his bride.

Spear strikes his shoulder,
And he gasps aloud in sudden pain,
Urges the girl to faster swim,
Abena must not wait for him,
To follow her each sinew strains.

He does not see the floating log,
Until almost on top of him,
The log it is a crocodile,
Mouth opens in its ghastly smile,
Faster he attempts to swim.

Abena hears him shout and screams,
Sees the beast just miss his head,
Arms thrashing swims back to his side,
Jaws clamped on her, it downwards glides
to murky depths of river bed.

Kwame cries out in deep despair,
Repeated dives, shouting her name,
Those upon the bank now turn,
To their village sad return,
Her father bends his head in shame.

His daughter truly loved that man,
He realises this too late,
Abena would not now be dead,
Had he but truly used his head,
He sits there brooding at her fate.

Then seizes length of ebony,
Sits carving there long in the night,
His daughter tries to recreate,
Kwame can no longer hate,
Weariness now blurs his sight.
Runners come, call in his hut,
'Kwame, he died from loss of blood.
You are avenged our honoured Chief.'
But he just sits there in his grief,
Stares at Abena, carved in wood.

Years later, when that old chief died,
A trader to the village came,
Upon a shelf Abena stands,
Lifts figurine with reverent hands,
'Is she for sale, the sum just name?'

'Take him, man. Take Abena,
The chief who carved her is no more,
To honoured ancestors departed,
The old man he was broken hearted,
His action he did long deplore.'

The trader listened sombrely
That figurine was exquisite,
A woman he knew, with skilful hands,
About slender neck, place golden bands,
Jewels and dress upon her fit.

Maria sudden wakes and stares,
Eyes upon the carving played,
So much more than merest dream,
A precious vision it would seem,
Abena's life, death, just replayed.

Remembers the stall holder—Kofi,
He who had brought Abena here,
Now far from Africa's hot sun,
A secret life change just begun.
The carving she'd hold always dear.

A holiday now starts to plan,
To Gambia will make her way,
Search to find that jungle glade,
To stand beneath its dappled shade,
And Kofi—meet her there one day?

AFTERMATH

Shy as wild rose tipped with flame,
Beneath new risen sun,
The lassie kicked her shoes aside,
To step into the swirling tide,
Nor saw the redcoat lift his gun.

A sour grin spread upon his face,
He has her in his sight,
Adjusting musket on a boulder,
Butt is firm against his shoulder,
Prepares to press the trigger tight.

The lass kilted up her gown,
Dainty toes step in the brine,
Shudders to its cold embrace,
Tossing curls back from her face,
Moving, hears bullets whine.

In terror plunges in the sea,
Impeded by full skirted gown,
Strikes away from sandy shore,
Swiftly Prays God to implore,
Not to be wounded, nor yet drown.

The redcoat curses and reloads,
Then feels a hand his shoulder clamp,
His captain stares down in distaste,
'Fellow, you are a rank disgrace,
Get you back now to the camp.'

'We wage not war on women!'
'Why let them live to breed more foes.'
Truculent rises to his feet,
Then beats disconsolate retreat,
The captain watches as he goes.

Then turns his gaze upon the sea,
Sees the girl's dark bobbing head
Now some distance from the land.
He leaps down the cliff on to the sand,
In that strong tide she'll soon be dead.

The girl's dark head now disappears.
He tosses aside fine scarlet coat,
Into the cold autumnal tide,
Swims in attempt to reach her side,
If only there had been a boat.

He dives, the water not too deep,
 Twas here he saw her disappear,
Several attempts the captain makes,
One last dive despairing takes,
The girl perhaps in her last sleep.

But then his hand grasps her hair,
Determined pulls her up above,
Sees her white and lovely face,
Holds her in a firm embrace,
Faint tendrils now are born of love.

Strong legs strike out for the shore,
Gasping he pulls her on the sand,
Turns her on her shapely side,
She had so very nearly died,
He strokes her head with gentle hand.

She splutters as he forces out
Water from her protesting lungs,
Opening eyes of gentian blue,
Never had he seen such hue,
Wet waist long hair about her clung.

'Why did you save me?' lifts her head,
He shrugs and reaches for his coat,
Wraps her in its warmth of red,
'Where is your home,' quietly said,
Lifts strand of seaweed from her throat.

'My house is half a mile from here,
At least it was, but now destroyed,
King Georges men no warning gave,
My parents lie in new dug grave,
I hid, escaped, freedom enjoyed.'

'I am your prisoner it seems,
Sir, what your pleasure now with me.'
Slim, she rose on slender feet,
Her voice he heard, was low and sweet,
Lowering her head despondently.

'Lady I crave to know your name,'
'Roseanna Grant,' she soft replied,
'Caught up in all this cruel strife,
In which I nearly lost my life,
Where Scotland's finest sons have died.'

'I'm Captain John Brandon, my men await,
Where shall I take you pretty maid?
Some place of safety there must be,
Friends, relatives awaiting thee,
No need now to be afraid.'

'Yes, I know of a certain cave,
Situation fear I cannot tell,
There will I go and safety find,'
Glanced at his face, dark eyed and kind,
'Captain I now wish you farewell.'

He watched her lissom stride away,
His warm red coat now at his feet,
He shivered, stooped and put it on,
A dark hair round its button clung,
The memory of her very sweet.

The hills and glens ran red with blood,
Man and beast, none spared until
At last the enemy depart,
Leaving many an aching heart,
For those whom they had wanton killed.

Three years had passed on leaden feet,
Roseanna with great uncle lives
High in the hills they vigil keep,
That none steal their small flock of sheep,
Wool and sustenance these give.

A horseman rides into the hills,
Direction asks, demanding whether
Mistress Roseanna Grant lives near,
Of him she has no cause to fear,
Horse takes a path amongst the heather.

John Brandon sees her winsome face,
Wind blowing through dark chestnut hair,
She sees him and draws back in fright,
The sun now sinking into night,
Wonders what he is doing there.

'Roseanna,' he holds out his hand,
She approaches on distrustful feet,
'My dear, I had to come,' he said,
'Ask that you share my board and bed,
Sweet wife become I now entreat.'

'John Brandon, where's your coat of red,'
'Like my past life it's cast aside,
An end put to military career,
Three years I've longed for you my dear,
Now humbly ask you be my bride.'

As the soft winds of beauteous Skye,
Swept over slopes of fragrant heather,
Two enemies, now foes no more,
Stole down upon that sandy shore,
John satisfied in his endeavour.

With kind and all forgiving heart,
Her uncle his permission grants,
John and Roseanna now are wed,
A small cot provides their marriage bed,
John Brandon's name now changed to Grant.

So may all enemies forswear
That which drives their lives apart,
Love than hate forever stronger,
Bringing hope and lasting longer,
Mankind so offered a new start.

CANDLE TO RUDI

Light a candle to Rudi,
Keep his memory green,
For today was his birthday,
His life now a dream.

I remember that bed sit,
Cherry blossom at Kew,
The births of our children,
And those trips to the zoo

All that work, 'menches kinding'
Fraught fraus and professors
Dedication, some drinking,
Long hours, mounting pressures.

But fix your eyes on the candle,
In the heart of its flame,
See the love and devotion,
Always the same.

See the courage and laughter,
So bright to the end,
Of a dearly loved father,
Liebchen and friend.

Light a candle to Rudi,
Let its flame ever glow,
In our hearts, who loved him,
And still do, here below.

The candle is melting,
But the love carries on,
In our writings and music,
Communications and song.

Each year light that candle,
Let its light steal above,
To the spirit of Rudi,
At peace in God's love.

SKYE MEMORIES

A drift of dreams steals over the hill,
From those high places where once we trod
Tumbling in the spangled lace of waterfalls,
Sighing in the salt sea wind.
Memories--tenuous as the wet sea mists,
That wrap the land in a swaddling
Robe of dreams.
Pale gold the Cuillins in the noon sun,
Close guarding the waters
On your grey sanded shore.
Black rocks embracing a sea
Whose colours change from pearl to
Turquoise, to softest amethyst.
Footprints swept clean by swift incoming tide.
Pebbles gleaming wetly in black and
Jade, palest pink and mauve.
Tangled seaweed, fragile shells.
Memories arising still--
As above, so below
Clouds above nestling above on peaks below,

Where Norsemen buried their
Dead princess.
Grassy cliffs-----wild orchids
Glowing pink, white and purple
In the young grass.
Dainty bluebells flinching to
The breeze. sprigs of early
Bell heather---thyme,
Blushing dog-rose and tall spires
Of dusky foxglove.
Yellow iris fringing the burn, whilst
On heather moor, dragon-flies
Skim, hover, and bog cotton
Ripples to the breeze.
Cry of gulls soaring the wind,
Bleat of sheep, sure-footed on the brae,
Splash of otter, bobbing seal,
Phantom call of the wild
Sea bull.
Golden eagle swooping down, down
From jagged peak.
Double rainbows loop the bay,
Iridescent---shimmering through

Scudding cloud.

Then evening----as islands hide in

Rose-tinted mist and sunset falls.

All these are Skye—of my long

Love------A sacred place

Within my mind.

DRUMBEAT OF LOVE – TO BYRON

Drumbeat of love,
How constant its message,
Heartbeat of compassion,
Searching all hearts,
Rhythm of courage,
Inquiring, demanding,
Answer to life's hurts-
Why no solace imparts.

Drumbeat of Love,
Guided by kindness,
Sure hands and steady,
In echoing beat,
Faster and faster,
Frustrated crescendo,
Pain and love blending
His song now complete.
Drumbeat of love,
It throbs yet among us,
Disturbing life's tenor,

Echoing through space,
Beloved young drummer,
At peace now in heaven
Precious memory forever
We yield to God's grace.

THE VISION

There was a man besieged by doubt,
That nightly crouched beside his bed,
Could it be true on point of death,
As man exhaled last laboured breath,
His spirit was not truly dead.

Wandering out beneath the stars,
Stared as he never had before,
Frost bright it shone that glittering haze,
He lowered troubled brooding gaze,
As now his lips wildly implore.

And you are real, pray hear my cry,
Satisfy my life long quest,
Beauty which doth my soul entrance,
Surely all is not wrought by chance,
But at Thine own awesome behest.

Mighty, mysterious Creator God,
Can it be true the Holy One,
Chose this earth of ours to grace,
That in Him we should see Your face,
Glimpse Father's glory in the Son.

Should I believe that from the tomb,
He walked once more the world of men,
Did he who died upon a cross,
Those myriad stars in heaven toss,
Expired—to truly rise again.

How do I know all is not myth,
He sighed, returned once more to bed,
From lips a whispered prayer arose,
His tired eyes about to close,
Widen in awe and sudden dread.

The vision fills his heart and mind,
Those wondrous eyes, questing, tender,
The nail scarred hand so gently raised,
The man his fearful gaze abased,
Trembling lips now worship render.

He rises to a radiant dawn,
Exultation floods his mind,
The demon doubt forever banished,
All last uncertainty now vanished,
New path in life resolves to find.

MOTH IN A MOONBEAM

Moth in a moonbeam,

Cough of hot lead,

Black holes in a hooded man's side.

As a rustling night wind,

Sighs were ye Protestant friend,

Or perhaps for the ould faith ye died.

Dew on a cobweb,

Blood on the grass,

And a car that speeds swift down the lane.

As a nightjar's harsh cry,

Echoes why, why and why,

So many in freedom's name.

Berry on briar bush,

Youth in a ditch,

And a crime that shrieks high to the sky.

As poor Ireland's soft green,

Daubed in crimson is seen,

But the painter he does not live nigh

The painter he does not live nigh!

SKYE COTTAGE

All night I wept a love now dead,
My pillow wet with sorrow's dew,
Impatient now, rise from my bed,
Up--up to face the world anew.

The sun so bright, I blink then stare,
At the strange beauty of this place,
Last night so blind in my despair
I'd walked past with averted face.

Now venturing from the cottage door,
Into a morn of glittering gold,
I turn my steps towards the shore,
Mere hundred yards from here, I'm told.

Bluebells flow about my feet,
Golden broom sways in the breeze,
Heart throbs with quick, enchanted beat,
Wind whipping dress about my knees.

At cliff's edge, pause in wondering awe,
As far below waves sweep the sand,
Foam tossed, slam their glistening flanks
Surging where ancient black rocks stand.

Gulls swoop and scream and sail the wind,
As cautious crouching I descend,
This grassy cliff where wild flowers cling
And orchids nestle, dip and bend.

Slither down the last few feet,
Clamber on pebbles mauve and black,
How fresh the air, salt laden, sweet.
I fill my lungs, straighten my back.

The sea is shimmering, shot with light,
Deep turquoise, green and amethyst,
Blue shadowed mountains guard the bay,
Sharp peaks enwrapped in drifting mist.

True I'd nursed a broken heart,
Pain searing deep, but now absurd,
A new love flooding every part.
Spirit ascending, like a bird.

New love born on these cliffs of Skye,
Now throbs its message in my breast
To stay with me until I die
A longing to give me no rest.

THE CHRISTMAS TREE

The mother held her tiny babe,
Towards the Christmas tree,
Cradled soft to loving breast,
And gaily laughed to see,
The dimpled fingers reach to touch,
The baubles shining bright,
Upon that glittering, tinselled tree,
Agleam with candle light.

Now sleep you soft, my precious babe,
Beneath the fragrant pine,
You'll always have a Christmas tree,
I promise, baby mine.

Three happy years sped swiftly by,
Till from a hospital bed,
The weary toddler fitful cried,
And shook her sweat-damp head.
Then smiled to see the fairy lights,
Upon the Christmas tree,
Nor saw the doctor shake his head,
In sad finality.

Now sleep you soft, my precious babe,
Beneath the fragrant pine,
You'll always have a Christmas tree,
I promise, baby mine.

The mother fastened candles white,
Into the spreading yew,
Soaring above the tiny grave,
Where grasses softly blew.
The waxen candles blazed with light,
On sparkling, frost kissed tree,
The mother set aside her light,
And knelt upon her knee.

Now rest you soft, my precious babe,

Beneath the fragrant pine,

You'll always have a Christmas tree,

I promise, baby mine.

MOONDUST

Midnight's lamp hangs palely
poised, soft outline smudged,
rainbow light pooling down
in shifting radiance
as phosphorescent waves,
prickle, toss and sway
glimmering with myriad
phantom fireflies.
Silver seals make wistful moan,
enjoined by surging rush of
swift incoming tide, sucking at pebbles,
slapping grey sand, advancing,
retreating, making night's music,
beneath frosted stars.
Harsh heather roots bruise
sandalled feet, sharp rocks impede, as
I pant upwards, ever upwards
to the cliff's edge. A shower of tiny
moths rise, flutter gauzy wings
shimmering with moon dust.

And I gaze with awe at this beauty

spread before my tear wet eyes.

What place man's small sorrows

encountering such tapestry

of light and dark, heaven's vault

awesome, huge, so remote.

Stygian heights above soaring incandescent

with planets, stars--glittering immensity!

How great it's Maker, the incomparable Artist!

Hurt—loss of love's dream,

all will fade. Yet this vision on the high

cliffs of Skye remain forever

jewelled memory within

my heart.

RIDERS IN THE NIGHT

The Cottage looked inviting,
I gave contented sigh,
Remote up here upon the moor,
Pale roses climbing round its door,
As crystal burn runs chuckling by.

White walls under old thatched roof,
Unlock the door and wander in.
In his last will and testimony,
Briar Cottage has been left to me
By Great Uncle Iain, distant kin.

Shelves are dusty, many books,
Old paintings hang upon the wall,
By staircase, ancient rocking chair,
I glance around with curious stare,
Brown velvet couch slightly recall.

In my not too distant youth,
My parents had once brought me here,
Great Uncle had warm welcome given,
This cottage seemed my childish heaven,
On memories page his voice rang clear.

'Annie, this place is right for you,'
His voice came echoing from the past,
Mother had listened at a loss,
'Her name is Jane,' her voice was cross,
My father looked strangely aghast.

They let him take me on the moor,
His silver hair and beard wind tossed
Hard work worn hand closed over mine,
Wise old eyes with fervour shine,
That peat brown burn swung me across.

We clamber up a rock strewn hill,
Prickled with sea of golden gorse,
Dance at his side through heather clumps,
Watch laughing, as he slaps the rump
Of whinnying devoted horse.

Mounting pulls me up before him,
We gallop down along the lane,
That runs across that heather moor,
Strange memories of times of yore
Filtered through, my childish brain.

Next day we left in dusty Ford,
Great Uncle waved beside his door,
They never brought me back again,
As though some unresolved pain,
My anxious parents did deplore.

Now they were dead, Great Uncle too,
A writer now was my profession,
Around the world my novels sell,
Financially I've done quite well,
Yet sometimes suffer from depression.

A hidden place within my mind.
Sometimes I feel an inner rage,
Try as I may and often do,
Deep buried incidents to view,
Cannot unlock far memories cage.

I sweep and dust, unpack my case,
Open windows, let in the light,
Scent of bell heather fills the air,
Open my laptop and prepare
To sit, relax, perhaps to write.

But first I stoop and light the stove,
Smell of wood smoke and of peat,
A kettle sings out merrily,
I make a welcome cup of tea,
At Iain's table take my seat.

So many times had he sat thus,
Staring out across the moor,
Tried to recall his craggy face,
Memories fading into space,
Until at last I try no more.

Restless rise up to my feet,
Walk to those shelves of dusty books,
Lifted one up, stared curiously,
Name of its author then struck me,
Deep breath of amazement took.

Iain MacLeod—Great Uncle then,
Had been an author just like me,
I dropped into the rocking chair,
For long hours I sat reading there
Tale of sad love and mystery.

That novel read to final page,
Put it aside with troubled look,
The young girl Annie featured there,
With tawny eyes and russet hair,
Reality leapt from the book.

I lit the lamps and bolt the door,
Of sudden feeling quite alone,
The sun sinks down below the hill,
Approaching night so very still,
Its soft wind making faintest moan.

The sheets are cold about my legs,
Blankets damp but I crave sleep,
Feather pillows neath my head,
I snuggle down into the bed,
Sigh, fall into slumber deep.

What was that, eyes open wide,
I sit bolt upright in the bed,
Look around in sudden fright,
Shouts and screams sully the night,
I tremble there in growing dread.

I hear the sound of horses' hooves,
Trot-trot, trot-trotting down the lane,
Hear shots, the curtains draw aside,
The moon pools silver light outside,
Unknown girl grasps her horse's mane.

Curiosity stronger now than fear,
Unbolt the door and slip outside,
Pale beneath soft shifting moonlight,
The rider now in desperate flight,
The gown she wears that of a bride.

A man black bearded, fierce of face,
Has grasped the bridle, horse now rears,
While on the ground, close to its feet,
A wounded, bloodstained man entreats,
As horse rears, bolts and disappears.

The fierce assailant gives a roar,

His own horse mounts, rides in pursuit,

The wounded man attempts to rise,

I see his face, gasp in surprise,

Iain MacLeod shot by that brute.

Great Uncle Iain's face was young,

Yet he it was, without a doubt,

His wedding suit is stained with gore,

'Annie, ride fast,' his voice implores

'My brother's a cruel, dastardly lout.'

His fingers claw at heather roots,

Again tries desperate to arise,

Staggers unsteady to his feet,

Never to accept defeat,

'You dare to touch her,' his voice defies.

Stumbling follows after them,

On strange light feet, I speed ahead,

Those riders gallop up a hill,

Annie's horse outruns him still,

Hands grasp its mane, gives it its head.

A chasm opens ugly mouth,
Beneath a burn rages in spate.
Don MacLeod gives warning scream,
Her eyes in desperation gleam,
Horse leaps, surrendering to its fate.

Far, far below, the horse and girl,
Are swept away by raging tide,
Don MacLeod stares brooding down,
He had not meant the lass to drown,
Had hungered for his brother's bride.

He turns, spurs off into the night,
Iain now married has no wife,
A widower with sorrow laden,
For his lovely red haired maiden,
To grieve for her throughout his life.

An accident most thought it was,
The horse with that young bride had bolted,
True to his oath, doctor refrained,
Iain's injuries to explain,
Some curious rumours at last halted.

The visions faded, sudden chill,
Forced me once more to seek my bed,
To brood on now established fact,
My own grandfather's savage act,
Had left Great Uncle's Annie dead.

I wondered why he had not spoken,
Exposed his brother's heinous crime,
Perhaps strange family loyalty,
Allowed my grandfather go free,
Such decency surely sublime.

Next day I wondered on the hill,
Found that dread spot where she had died,
No horse could e'er that chasm leap,
Where Annie fell to her last sleep,
As death this lovely bride surprised.

Drawn to the little village Kirk,
In quiet garden saw two graves,
Annie and Iain lay at rest,
Spirits residing with the blessed,
Tear damp my eyes, a deep sigh gave.

Return to the cottage, read again
That novel bearing Iain's name,
He'd changed the names I realised,
This method uncle had devised,
To expose his brother's shame.

The truth of Annie's tragic death,
I understood from Iain's book,
They'd wed, rode back from the Kirk,
In jealous rage with gun and dirk,
Don following the path they took.

Attacked his brother, Iain fell,
Annie to escape had desperate tried,
The rest I'd seen in waking dream,
Beneath the half moon's fitful gleam,
When Iain lost his lovely bride.

To Canada Grandfather sailed,
Married and had fine sons three,
One wed my mother, who gave birth
To me and then Scotland's dear earth
Called to us across the sea.

When I was five we made a visit,
Great Uncle stared long and hard at me,
Seems I reminded him of Annie,
She who could have been my granny,
Over the years remembered me.

Perhaps my long, straight, red gold hair,
Had struck a chord within his heart,
His lovely cottage left to me,
His books I'll treasure reverently,
From Briar Cottage never part.

The wind blows sweetly on the heath,
Pours down from that strange rugged hill,
Where rushing burn sad memory holds,
Of night beneath that moonlight cold,
Annie's cries, some hear them still.

EDINAMPLE COTTAGE

There's a cot in the Highlands,
That my heart will aye yearn,
Nestling soft in Glenample,
Above fair Loch Earn.
Around it soar mountains,
Their peaks lifting high,
In a landscape whose beauty
Enchanteth the eye.

A wild rushing burn,
Surges swift past my door,
Its waterfall sounding
Mellifluous roar,
Peaceful sheep in the meadow,
Phantom deer on the hill,
As twilight falls softly
And tall pines hang still.

Now moon gleams mysterious,
Through cloud shapes of time,
Whilst the wind shakes the trees,
In furious mime.
Tossing memories of past deeds,
In this wild lonely glen,
And of women who wept
For their wild Highland men.

If the hills could but speak,
What a story they'd tell,
Of their sons and daughters,
Who lived neath their spell,
As centuries sped by,
Like a twinkling of light,
From the shimmering stars,
In the bright, frosty night.

Loch Earn's lovely waters,

Slap hard on the shore,

Glinting dull neath the moonlight,

In valley's deep floor,

There to dream, until dawn's flame,

Bright flushes the sky

And a blackbird trills sweetly,

That morning is nigh.

A morning of rainclouds,

A flurry of snow,

Then bright gold on the hills

And a vivid rainbow-----

Wistful brilliance of jewelled hues,

Looping the bay,

As the cottage stands snug,

To another new day.

Edinample------a haven
From worlds weary storm,
Where a wanderer on life's road,
Feels sheltered and warm
You're an answer to prayer,
On that long road I've trod,
A dream now fulfilled,
By an all caring God.

Soon summer will come,
Rhododendrons will bloom,
Sweet wild flowers be woven
On Nature's fair loom.
Shifting sunlight will filter
Through whispering trees,
And then, even as now,
I will fall on my knees.

Lifting heart, hands and voice,
To that Almighty King,
Whose praises and glory,
Forever I'll sing.

HYMN OF PRAISE

How great and glorious art Thou
Oh God, our Father—who hast
girded earth with night's
starry mantle----shimmering infinity
beyond grasp of our
small minds.
How beautiful thy works, Great Artist.
How wondrous thy brush strokes
upon the clouds of dawn.
Who can match thy palette, Lord-----
damp, suffused pearl, rising from
breast of swelling sea—surmounted by peach light
till all lies joined in glittering
heart of gold.
How gentle Thy touch,
which sets translucent
bell of convolvulus, in thrusting
hedgerow---pale trumpets, raised
in praise.

How gracious Thy love, opening our wistful
nostrils to sweetness of rose and honeysuckle,
essence of beauty-----fragrance
of tenderness.
How soft Thy hand, smoothing feathers
of new fledged thrush, giving it's throat
to melody of praise.
A praise for all things, Mighty One.
For sparkle of clear water, between rocks,
spraying down from wooded crag, to
join broad river.
For swaying green of towering trees,
earth's own cathedral-----
dappled light, filtering twixt leaves,
each quivering blade of grass beneath,
whispering Thy praise-----Thy glory!
Cloud shapes, dulling the gold of
ripening corn, as wind pouring sweetly
murmurs---remember--
always remember
of whom each swelling grain
is wrought!

All thy earth lives in
ever present praise
of Thee----each tiny minnow—each small
green croaking frog—
each dripping otter---each mighty eagle,
soaring towards Thy infinite heart.

We tremble at Thy lightning flash—the
thundering of Thy wrath between
the hills of time.
How great Thou art---how awesome------yet gave
Thine own sweet Son to bear
our sin on cruel wood, that once sprang
from seed fallen upon the earth---as did
His dear blood so fall in healing grace---in
Mystery of love----resurrection of
Light, to guide the footsteps
of mankind!
Praise Thee, Father---
Praise Thee, Beckoning Way----
Praise Thee, Spirit.

ROCK MY DARLING, ROCK

The mother softly placed her babe,
In that old wooden cot,
Smiled down into her bright blue eyes,
Blue as forget-me-nots.
Now rock my darling, rock my darling
Rock my darling, rock.

The little girl sat on the swing,
Then gasped as it flew higher,
My darling do you see that plane,
One day you'll be a flyer.
So fly my darling, fly my darling,
Fly my darling, fly.

The young bride smiled in his embrace,
Responding to his kiss.
Entered loves sweet rhythm then,
In joy of married bliss.
Rock my darling, rock my darling,
Rock my darling, rock.

The widow looked down at the grave,
Her children at her side,
They placed their flowers as she recalled
Those days as happy bride.
Sigh my darling, sigh my darling,
Sigh my darling, sigh.

The frail form in the rocking chair,
Her eyes a faded blue,
Smiled and gripped its arms to rock,
As she now loved to do.
Rock my darling, rock my darling,
Rock my darling, rock.

STORM CLOUDS

Dark storm clouds mask the evening sky,
Fast rushing to eternity,
They bear the anguish of my cry,
My yearning, aching need of thee.

Wild waves crash sullen on the shore,
Their dying ebb like passion spent,
Within their depths I'd feel no more,
Their tumult still my heart's lament.

But what if in that surging tomb,
My restless spirit found no peace,
But rose up from the water's gloom,
To wander earthbound without cease,

Until life's own relentless stream,
Heals all pain in oblivion's dream.

GOING HOME

A land of mystery, old as time,
Forever beckoning me.
Scent of grey gums, wafts through my mind,
Dredging deep memories.

Flash of an axe on Lightning Ridge,
Opals shimmering desire,
Red desert ablaze with wild flowers of spring,
Starlit nights of drowsing desire.

Those calls that come ghosting through the trees,
As a huge moon pools pale light,
A bounding shape disappearing with ease,
Into the warm, pulsing night.

A dawn that gashes the sky with flame,
Pouring purple and gold on the hills,
Fish that challenge in waiting game,
My rod poised watchful and still.

Tall reeds fringing rivers deep yellow flow,
Croaking frogs by still, green pool.
Harsh songed birds, whose vivid colours glow,
Koalas playing the fool.

A mate who will take you for what you are,
Nor question your right to go
When restlessness beckons with wandering star,
As the camp fire burns down low.

All this lies again within my reach,
Across a welcoming sea.
Where the white breakers pound the sun scoured beach,
As my own land waits for me.

Written for my dear son Wernher, as I launch him with love, back to the land of his heart.
Mum xxx!

ONLY A MAN

I did not see an enemy,
I only saw a man.
Grey eyes met blue, an answering smile,
Our love affair began.

A war had ripped the world apart,
On inexorable tide.
Now tossed upon the shores of peace,
We stood there side by side.

We talked, nor wondered at the fate,
That drew us there together,
The knot of love soon to be tied,
Time alone would sever.

Captured in war, a prisoner
Of your own loss and pain.
Your country sundered in defeat,
How then to start again.

In a Hampshire country village,
Where suspicion still held sway,
A German and an English girl,
Danced and talked the night away.

Falteringly you spoke to me,
As I tried to understand,
How war had swept you from your village,
To many a distant land.

You longed once more to see your home
Upon the Baltic Sea.
But it had gone, now Polish folk
Lived in that territory.

The past now lay in ruins,
The future hard to see,
But love reached out a beckoning hand,
Forged bond twixt you and me.

No more an alien country,
Soon to become your own.
Four lovely children healed the wound
That hate and war had sown.

So you who read this story,
May compassion flood your heart,
Ignore inflammatory words
Which make new conflicts start.

To the stranger in your village
Reach out a welcoming hand,
No matter creed or colour,
Or from what distant land.

So do not see, an enemy.
Instead just see a man,
Or woman or a little child,
Their lives within God's plan.

TARMACHAN RIDGE

Tarmachan—Tarmachan,
Brooding, majestic,
Peaks wreathed in cloud silk,
Beneath a bruised
Sky.
Threads of pearl mist,
Your steep slopes descending,
Down drifting through
Bracken, soft as a
Sigh.

Browsing sheep snatching,
At wet golden grasses,
Snarled coats heavy,
With the fine, drenching
Rain.
Above all, a rainbow,
Wistful, translucent,
As shafts of thin sunlight,
Lance down once
Again.

Tarmachan—Tarmachan,
To the west, Lawers flanks you,
Gaunt shoulders raised,
Dark dreaming,
Serene.
Close guarding deep waters,
Tay's shifting radiance,
Milk mist, soft clinging,
To wavelets pale
Sheen.

Forest and mountain,
The Dochart's wild raging,
Rapids exploding,
Crash under the
Bridge.
Coppered trees dripping.,
Motionless, mist wrapped,
Brooding neath mystery,
Of Tarmachan
Ridge.

THE THORNBUSH

A thorn bush blooms amidst the snow,
Pale petals shining bright.
Its fragrance reaching to the stars,
This very special night.
It breathes a wistful message from,
Its shimmering, windswept heart,
Perhaps a humble thorn bush,
One day will play its part.

My flowers are insignificant,
Yet as the angels sing,
My thorns prepare eternal crown,
For the new born baby King
Shepherds kneel in adoration,
The heavens flood with light,
All nature seems to hold its breath,
In wonder and delight.

The Son of God, in Mary's arms,

Sleeps sweetly unconcerned.

As Heaven's messengers proclaim,

The One man long has yearned.

Now the thorn bush droops it branches,

Sadly reflecting how,

Its sharp thorns will encircle,

The Christ Child's tender brow.

But twixt blossom and the prickle,

Everlasting life is born.

The thorn bush lifts its petals on,

That radiant Christmas morn,

Knowing Heaven's royal diadem,

Gleaming jewel bright,

Will replace its sharp tipped crown of thorns,

Drawing mankind to The Light.

THE BALALAIKA

The girl wore black.

Slim limbs encased in

Leather.

Lips red as

Balalaika

He watched her

As she stroked

Melancholy into

The night.

The bar was crowded,

Men tossed back tankards

Of foaming beer

The girl unnoticed.

One man did approach

Leered suggestively

To be ignored.

'Walk you home,'

He suggested.

Reached out

Eager hand.

She turned

Icy stare upon him.

Brought fingers fiercely

Across balalaika

Sound harsh,

 Discordant,

Causing drinkers pause.

Falteringly the man

Drew back

Surely, this woman

Was merely

Lady of the night

So-called.

He hesitated

Knowing all

Eyes upon him

Made new attempt.

'I pay well

My little pigeon.'

Again reached out

Desirous hand.

She lowered the

Balalaika.

Her fingers

Produced a knife
From slim belted
Waist.
She spoke no word
None needed.
He cursed
Turned away
Loud laughter attended
His confusion.
'She knows how to
Use it,'
one man confided,
rolled back his sleeve
exposing vivid scar
'None know her
Name.
But her music
Stirs the heart.
So listen,
enjoy.'
He drew back.
And once more
The girl lifted her
Red balalaika.

Printed in Great Britain
by Amazon